A HALO PUBLISHING INTERNATIONAL ANTHOLOGY

The Journey is the Gift

THE MOMENT THAT CHANGED MY STORY

Halo
PUBLISHING
INTERNATIONAL

Halo
PUBLISHING
INTERNATIONAL

Halo Publishing International
8000 W Interstate 10, #600
San Antonio, Texas 78230

First Edition, April 2023
Printed in the United States of America
ISBN: 978-1-63765-357-9
Library of Congress Control Number: 2023900155

The information contained within this book is strictly for informational purposes. Unless otherwise indicated, all the names, characters, businesses, places, events and incidents in this book are either the product of the author's imagination or used in a fictitious manner. Any resemblance to actual persons, living or dead, or actual events is purely coincidental.

Halo Publishing International is a self-publishing company that publishes adult fiction and non-fiction, children's literature, self-help, spiritual, and faith-based books. We continually strive to help authors reach their publishing goals and provide many different services that help them do so. We do not publish books that are deemed to be politically, religiously, or socially disrespectful, or books that are sexually provocative, including erotica. Halo reserves the right to refuse publication of any manuscript if it is deemed not to be in line with our principles. Do you have a book idea you would like us to consider publishing? Please visit www.halopublishing.com for more information.

Acknowledgements

We extend our heartfelt gratitude to every individual
who has made a contribution to this book

Roberto Alfaro

Susan Eileen

Natalie Zangara Friedl

Scarlett Green-Wright

Crista Salvatore

Cammie Smith

Sabrina VanDine Smith

Lisa Michelle Umina

Natalie Wintle

Contents

Dear Readers,

We are thrilled to present to you our book, **The Journey is the Gift: The Moment that Changed My Story**. This anthology is a collection of meaningful and transformative experiences from individuals who refused to dodge life's curves. The authors in this book have faced challenging and life-altering moments, from near-fatal accidents to unexpected motherhood, but have emerged stronger and more resilient.

Through their stories, you will see those changes, no matter how unexpected or difficult, can shape us into better versions of ourselves. The authors embody vibrant transformations and remind us that our will to keep living and thriving beyond just coping is itself the miracle.

We hope that this book will inspire and encourage you on your own journey. It serves as proof that no matter what curve life throws at us, it is possible to overcome and find meaning in the journey.

Sincerely,

Lisa M. Umina
CEO & Award-Winning Author

Our Authors

> **Never Stop Dreaming, because No Dream Is Too Big to Dream!**

1

The Invention That Changed My Life and the Life of Others Forever

Roberto Alfaro

Way before becoming a published author, I was living my lifelong dream as a police officer. For twenty-one dedicated years, I proudly served the City of Hartford, Connecticut, until my retirement in 2000. Saving lives and making a difference in the community I worked for, was one of the most rewarding and amazing experiences of my life. As someone who grew up poor in one of the worst drug and gang-infested neighborhoods of the South Bronx during the '60s and '70s, I certainly knew firsthand the importance of dreaming big and never giving up on your goals of living a better and more fulfilling life than the one offered by the tough environment that surrounded me every day.

Besides living in a dangerous neighborhood riddled with crime, I was also living a nightmare at home. My father was a violent alcoholic who at times had us running from our home in fear of our lives, seeking shelter in the middle of the night. This went on for many, many years and left behind a slew of traumatic memories, which took me numerous years to overcome, especially as a young child.

At school I was also bullied, from kindergarten to fourth grade, until one day when I got beaten so badly by a bully that I ended up in the emergency room. After that horrible experience, my older brother took me under his wing and taught me how to box.

Learning to protect myself proved to be one of the biggest turning points of my life; I was never bullied again. I suddenly went from this extremely shy kid who barely spoke a word in class and had no friends, to a kid who had tons of friends and quickly found himself going down the wrong road, hanging around with the wrong people. By the age of fourteen, I was already a high school dropout with an uncertain future ahead of me. Through the grace of God, several amazing mentors came into my life at just the right time, and they were able to put me back on the right track. Before long, I found myself graduating from high school, and I ultimately became the first person in my family to go to college.

Later in life, I would go on to fulfill my lifetime dream of becoming a police officer. Not only did I become a decorated officer, but years later I became a mounted police officer and instructor. Other dreams soon followed, and before I knew it, I was a professional model and actor, a salsa dancer and instructor, a personal trainer and bodybuilding champion, a motivational speaker, an inventor, a writer, and, finally, the published author of my memoir, *Fighting through the Hurdles of My Life.*

In chapter one of my book, I share a story of how so many of these wonderful accomplishments and dreams in my life would have never happened had it not been for an unexpected miracle and blessing from God, which ultimately saved my life and eventually put me on the path to saving infants' lives with my invention!

When I was a baby, I suffered a health crisis. I started crying uncontrollably for hours on end. This was followed by constant bouts of extremely high fever, vomiting, and diarrhea. Because of this, I ended up in the emergency room. The persistent vomiting continued throughout the day, to the point that I could no longer hold anything in my stomach. In the hours that followed, I took a turn for the worse and ended up in a coma for three to four days, according to my parents. According to the doctors, all my symptoms were caused by what they described then as an unknown, serious E. coli-type bacterial stomach virus that had taken control of my body. My chances of survival that night looked extremely grim.

However, through it all, my parents refused to give up hope. They prayed by my bedside for those three to four grueling days, all in hopes that I would somehow, someway overcome this debilitating condition and suddenly awaken from the coma. Thanks to God's blessings, their prayers were answered. On the fourth day of being in that dire condition, I slowly but surely started showing signs of regaining consciousness.

Over the days and hours that followed, I started showing positive signs of improvement. I eventually was able to wake up completely and steadily improve, so much so that I was released from the hospital after a couple of weeks, and went on to live a normal and healthy life. It was a true miracle, according to the doctors and my parents. Because of that miracle, I am blessed to be here today to share my story.

Growing up, I always had this vision of paying the miracle forward somehow; I just didn't know how or when. During my twenty-one years of service, I was able to make a difference in the lives of others. However, it wasn't until years later, after I retired from the police force, that I came up with an invention that I knew in my heart and soul would one day prevent infant deaths due to being left in hot cars.

On August 18, 2018, I created Hooked on Baby and posted my invention on Facebook. In my lengthy post, I also included a video demonstration of how my invention works and information about how cost-effective it was to purchase the necessary items online, emphasizing that, by doing so, lives of infants would be saved. Here's my Facebook post from that day:

> *Throughout my many years as a public servant, nothing has been more painful to watch (or hear about) in the national news than when you hear of an infant (or child) dying as a result of a tragic accident. Such is the case when it involves babies dying from a case of heatstroke in a hot car after accidentally being left behind by a parent or guardian. And, sadly, as first responders, we're usually the first ones at the scene of such tragic outcomes and in the end ultimately in charge of investigating and dealing with such heartbreaking tragedies. Scenes like these can have a lasting effect on all first responders. This is especially true if the investigating officers also happen to be parents or grandparents themselves…and that's when it really hits home and tears at your heart.*
>
> *In just this year (2018) alone, 29 infant deaths have been attributed to babies being left in hot cars. And according to the national stats on infant car deaths, more than 400 hundred infants have died from being*

left in a hot car in the last 10 years, amounting to an average of about 39 infant deaths a year.

One day, highly determined and inspired to make a difference in the lives of these innocent babies, I sat at home and did a lot of brainstorming, research, and eventually drafting a rough diagram of my idea on paper. By the end of the day, I was blessed to come up with this invention (idea) that I hoped and prayed would ultimately make a difference and save lives. I decided to call it Hooked on Baby! Because, with this invention, that's basically what you are—you are physically connected to your baby by way of a lifeline. In essence, Hooked on Baby serves as a lifeline between you and your baby!

The video and still photos that I shared on my post clearly showed that by connecting three totally separate items, I was able to create Hooked on Baby. The idea is to connect your baby's car seat to you or to any personal item in your car, such as a backpack, purse, or even the belt loop of your pants. This creates a bonding connection between you and your infant. Then when you try to leave the vehicle, or grab your personal items to exit your vehicle, Hooked on Baby tugs at you and forces you to look back at your baby before unhooking yourself.

It went viral! That day, my post reached thousands and thousands of people, and I immediately knew that this was something very, very special. Over the days that followed my post, hundreds of inspiring comments and accolades came from concerned parents and grandparents who loved the idea and thought it was a much-needed solution to the large number of children in America who die each year after being left in hot vehicles. One parent wrote, "Great solution to a truly heartbreaking problem!" Another parent wrote, "This is a great idea; most people think, 'It won't happen to me. I will never forget my child in the back.' Then they forget. So please, everyone who has a little one, please get this! It may be one of us who forgets!" Another comment encouraged everyone to purchase my invention and said, "This will save the life of your child, grandchild, friend's child, or anyone's child!" The comments went on and on…too many to list!

I think that the best thing about this invention is that for less than ten dollars, you can purchase all of these items separately online—a Velcro strap, a forty-eight-inch retractable key chain, and a spring link—and have the comfort and peace of mind to know that, as long as you're both connected through the Hooked on Baby system, you will never forget your baby in the car. It is so simple to use, inexpensive, and, most importantly, very effective when used properly and on a daily basis!

This is just my personal plea and journey to save infant lives! My intent was never to make any money whatsoever on this. It's about saving lives!

All in all, my journey and the many hurdles I've had to overcome in my life were extremely difficult and even gut-wrenching at times. But somehow, someway, I always found the inner strength and determination to persevere against all odds. I did this by barreling through the many obstacles that tried to hold me back or veer me off-track. Luckily, I never, ever lost hope of making it one day and being successful. Through it all, I visualized myself accomplishing all these dreams. Overcoming setbacks. Staying the course. Thinking positively. Believing in myself. And, most importantly, never setting limits on what I could, or couldn't do in life.

It is this drive that I credit most of all for making me into the person that I am today. A success story of someone who never gave up on his dreams, even when everything around me was screaming, "Failure!" Thankfully, I never paid any mind to those negative voices that tried to alter my dreams. In the end, my hope is that by sharing my story and journey, I can inspire others to believe in themselves and never give up on their dreams and aspirations in life. For there is one thing that I know sure, and that is, if I could make it with all the hardships, heartbreaks, and tough times I faced, so can anyone! I am certainly living proof of that!

Here's a personal quote from one of my poems that serves as an inspiration in everything I do in my life. This motto has worked for me, and it can work for you as well!

Never Stop Dreaming, because No Dream Is Too Big to Dream!

*For more information about my invention, please Google "Public Safety Officer Invents Hooked on Baby." That link will take you to the *Quinnipiac Chronicle* article, which was published September 23, 2018, about my invention.

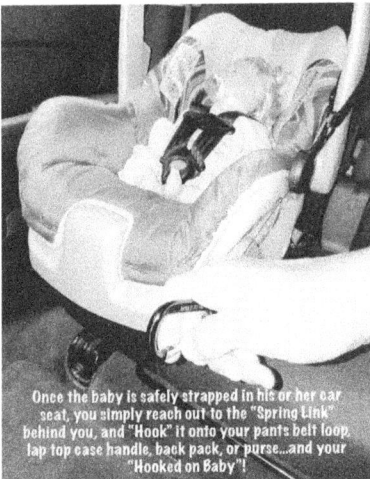

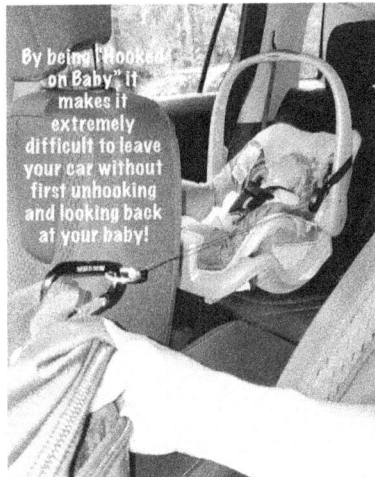

Once the baby is safely strapped in his or her car seat, you simply reach out to the "Spring Link" behind you, and "Hook" it onto your pants belt loop, lap top case handle, back pack, or purse...and your "Hooked on Baby"!

By being "Hooked on Baby" it makes it extremely difficult to leave your car without first unhooking and looking back at your baby!

66

I've learned that you have to
be very mindful about getting
better. There are no shortcuts.

99

2

Dying by the Numbers

Susan Eileen

Ninety thousand people died of fentanyl addiction in the last year. A teenager went to the emergency room in the midst of a mental breakdown; he waited twenty-seven days for a bed. A young woman went into a psychiatric hospital instead of killing herself; she got a bill for eighteen thousand dollars. Dissociative identity disorder is debilitating but extremely rare, affecting fewer than one percent of the population; those suffering from it are unable to function in the general population. These are just some of the stories in the news today.

Depression, PTSD, addiction—these invisible disabilities and patients are dying by the numbers, dying in silence. No faces, too many to count, too long forgotten to be remembered—just like the numbers of war. It is a war. It's a war on mental health in a system that is grossly incompetent when dealing with mental illnesses. Jails, institutions, and death—these are the inevitable ends of these cases. Lives gone far too soon. The diseases are shouting, but we are only equipped to deal with whispers.

This story, I hope, will serve as a cautionary tale for anyone who has yet to experience the "yets" of addiction and its exacerbating effect on mental illness. I haven't been to the psych ward *yet*. I haven't been to jail *yet*. I haven't been arrested *yet*. If you are telling yourself you don't have a problem because you are doing better than those with whom you are comparing yourself, consider those things that are still within the realm of possibility.

My absolute worst decision I have made to date was choosing to associate with someone who let me drink as much as I wanted to drink. The result was alcohol-induced psychosis. It landed me in a psychiatric facility on four occasions. I probably should have been institutionalized more, but there is a stigma attached to having been in a psychiatric facility. It was, however, the best thing that ever happened to me. I learned so much, but I kept running into the same people. There were ladies in the hospital whom I knew from rehab, my neighborhood, and even work. If that doesn't prove that this is a societal issue, then I don't know what does.

I met all kinds of people during my third trip to the psych ward. Under the advice of numerous people who claimed I wasn't bipolar, I abruptly stopped taking my medication. Let me tell you something I learned the hard way. Don't let people who are not doctors convince you that they know you better than you know yourself. It's insulting really. Furthermore, it's frustrating; these are the same people who recognize you are having serious problems managing adult life, but when you tell them the doctor's diagnosis, they disagree with it. They are not doctors. Don't take the armchair advice of your friends.

I learned so many things in the hospital, the most important being that after you've lost touch with reality once, it is very easy for it to happen again. You have to be very intentional about your progress and getting help. There are some small lifestyle adjustments you can make to help calm your mind. Your environment is crucial to getting better. Your lights should be as dim as possible, for instance, if you are overly excitable. Think of a sensory deprivation tank. They exist for a reason. Even the colors in your home influence you. Color theory, too, exists for a reason. Red is known to cause excitement, and blue is known to be calming. Use these ideas to your advantage.

As I said, upon the advice of several people, I went off my medication cold turkey. This caused a severe manic episode and detachment from reality. Things got so bad I was tempted to harm myself or others, so I called 911 on myself. Separating from reality was the scariest thing that ever happened to me. If I had acted upon my urges, I would now be in prison for life, criminally insane, or dead. Fortunately, some small part of me still knew right from wrong, and between the drugs and my untreated mental illness, I had turned into a menace to society.

Manic episodes are not well understood by people who don't have them. Depression, the other side of being bipolar, gets a lot more attention, but mania can be just as destructive and dangerous. When I'm manic, I'm hypersexual, I want to spend money as if it were going out of style, and I crave addictive substances. In short, my primitive brain goes wild. A common trait of mania is that you are also convinced that you are going to be the next millionaire. So you spend in advance of that, counting your chickens before they hatch. Ultimately, many people end up bankrupt and homeless, but still thinking they have the next get-rich-quick scheme, which ultimately, of course, goes nowhere.

Bipolar rage is also very hard to control. There is no impulse control when you are manic, bitter, and drinking. In the throes of bipolar rage, I sent copious texts to my ex-husband. To my mind, it was well-intentioned. I was trying to avoid a long, drawn-out legal case, but in reality it was harassment.

I was charged with telecommunications harassment, which landed me in probate court, where I was assigned a guardian ad litem. In short, it was a shit show.

Guardians ad litem are normally reserved for children in divorce cases. Here I was, a forty-seven-year-old woman, almost homeless, going to a state doctor for medications reserved for people who literally have no shoes, and being probated and assigned a guardian ad litem for supervision of my basic needs.

Probate court, though, was the first step in the right direction. There I met a man who looked as if he had been soaking in vodka since the universe was nine, women with conspiracy theories, and angry judges. And there I was, nodding out because I was still using. This was in 2018; I would not quit drinking until 2019, when I reached my breaking point and realized my next stop was death or prison. Even while high, these memories were burned into my brain. My last drink or illicit drug use was on December 9, 2019. I'd finally had enough of drinking, drugging, drug court, and dying young.

The last year of my addiction did land me in institutions, psychiatric facilities, and almost the cemetery. Ankle bracelets, straitjackets, judges, a swollen liver, and alcohol-induced seizures—that's where my addiction took me. I was unemployable. I couldn't hold a job or pay my bills; I was having seizures. But I finally decided to get sober, and now, a little more than three years out, I have been restored to sanity.

I realize that I have been discussing interchangeably both addiction and mental illness, but they are comorbid; they feed off one another. I was diagnosed with bipolar disorder in 1999. At that time, doctors only treated the symptoms, not the underlying problem, and realistically that is where things took a turn for the worse for me. I was in a manic episode and left the doctor's office with a prescription for Xanax. I was not given any healthy coping skills, and pills do not teach skills.

I started taking the prescriptions as directed, at first. Just one to fall asleep, nothing more. Eventually one pill wouldn't do, so I had to add in a beer. Then I needed two beers. The slippery slope began, and about six years later I was doctor shopping. I would fill three different prescriptions, from three different doctors, at three different pharmacies. I think, because I was a well-groomed teacher in the suburbs, it was easier to get away with it. I didn't look like a drug addict... yet. In my mug shot, I looked like an addict.

The most noticeable difference, immediately after getting sober, was that it seemed as if I had given myself a pay raise. I was no longer spending money on alcohol, pills, ankle bracelets, lawyers, bar food, or gas to get to the bar. I was no longer buying drinks for people with whom I had nothing in common. I also had copious time on my hands. I had little money, so I had to brainstorm free activities to keep myself busy. The library was an invaluable resource. I could pick up books to read, use their computer to work on my resume, and even meet like-minded people at their evening events, like Socrates Café, which is a discussion group in which thoughts are exchanged on the topical ideas and events of the day. There is also an extensive park system in my area. I spent time in nature as I had also been outdoorsy as a child. I went on guided hikes, went birdwatching, and met old friends for coffee.

As I had hit a pretty deep rock bottom, I had plenty to do to get my affairs in order. My house looked unlivable. I had plenty of laundry to do and bills to sort out; I had my work cut out for me. I've met many people who claim they drink because there is nothing else to do, but that is a bold-faced lie. There are museums, mini-golf, and fishing at a local lake. The possibilities for spending your time are endless. In active addiction, your world becomes as small as the bottle you are drinking or taking pills from, so of course you think there is nothing to do.

With my newfound time and money, I have reinvented myself. I've become an author. I've moved out of my hometown, learned to quilt, started writing poetry, and made new friends. I still feel unemployable, as I have both a master's degree and a criminal record, but I've made great progress on reducing expenses, which is the other side of the balance sheet.

Once sober, I realized that I never had my own identity. I was always living in the shadow of something else—my mother, my career, and eventually my addiction. It's a journey from self-destruction to reconstruction. I feel fortunate to have gotten sober at all. Everyone gets sober eventually, but most do it inside a coffin.

Addiction and mental illness are both very complicated disorders that exist on a spectrum. We know now that almost nothing in life is black and white. Invisible disabilities and addiction have degrees of severity, ranging from mild to severe. Genes, traumatic circumstances, and environment play a major role in how debilitating these disorders can be. I've learned that you have to be very mindful about getting better. There are no shortcuts. You'll have to not only watch what you ingest, but also what you put into your mind. Restoring yourself to health and sanity, if you ever even had either of those things, requires intentionality and focus.

The good news is that, typically, positive momentum is greater than the initial drive to change. Good habits pick up speed in much the same way bad habits do. Your one-thousandth day of sobriety should be much easier than your first. The cravings lessen with time. At some point, you realize that the new life you have built for yourself is not worth a shot of Jameson, a line of cocaine, or a few pain pills. You know from experience, that that one shot of Jameson will more than likely lead you back to jails, institutions, or death.

My life has changed so radically in the past three years that my life in active addiction is starting to become a fuzzy memory. I look ten years younger, have extended my life expectancy by decades, and have money in the bank. More importantly, though, are the intangible aspects of my personality that have appeared. I'm reliable, I'm trustworthy, and I have integrity. When I say now that I'll only be gone for fifteen minutes while running an errand, it's a true statement. I'm not going to get arrested, have sex with a stranger, or end up committing the never-ending stream of bad decisions that happen in active addiction. My judgment is no longer impaired, and I have a sense of clarity and purpose again.

Countless people have a fear of missing out or of boredom when they get sober. I decided life was passing me by as I sat in my local bar. Every dream, goal, or ounce of dignity I ever had evaporated inside of that bottle. I told myself life was more exciting with a bottle of beer in my hand, but, really, life was as boring as it could get. Everywhere I went, that bottle of beer came with me. I voluntarily excluded myself from events where alcohol wasn't included, like art museums, family parties, and eventually work.

If you are struggling with mental illness, addiction, or both, please consult with a doctor before doing anything. Talk with your pastor, wife, husband, best friend, or even legal counsel. Contrary to popular belief, quitting is for winners. I know from experience. The streets won't miss you, but your future will; your children already do. It's better to live paycheck to paycheck than trap house to trap house. And, eventually, you'll discover who you really are under all those layers of booze. You can either get sober now or do it from inside a coffin.

"

It doesn't matter how many children you have, you can love them all—and that is exactly what God does! He loves us all.

"

3

The Secret of the Moment

Natalie Zangara Friedl

December 24, 2003

Sitting at Denny's in the postmidnight hours of Christmas morning, after a long night out, they had no idea what the next twenty-four hours would bring. The recent engagement and purchase of their first home together brought excitement about the new year and their future.

Distracted by something behind her, his eyes missed hers throughout their conversation. Curious, she turned to see a family of four eating in silence. The mom, eyes down, gently moved food around the plate with her fork. The dad smoked a cigarette, perhaps having already finished his meal. A teenage son with headphones on had his head leaning against the wall, leaving a gap between him and his father, through which she could see the face of a young boy shoveling pancakes into his mouth without much thought about the world around him.

As her eyes connected back with his, he nodded as if to understand her unspoken request. He rose from the table and found the server. They smiled at one another, proud that they could take part in a little giving so early on Christmas morning.

The family rose to leave and searched the smoky, boisterous restaurant for the people who had paid their tab. The family would never suspect that any of these patrons, young and smelling like a bar, would have bought their meal, especially not this young couple with no idea what it took to be a family.

As the family left the restaurant, headed home to perhaps a beautiful Christmas, or maybe an empty one, the young boy in his jammies turned back, meeting her eyes with his. His smile flashed at her, and something familiar lingered.

She knew that he knew it was they who had paid for their meal. She knew that she would never forget the feeling she had the moment that little boy looked at her. She saw God in his eyes.

On the way home, they talked about how they wanted to keep what happened at Denny's their little secret. I'm happy to let you in on that secret because, without it, my life would not have changed.

Later that Christmas night, while opening gifts at my mom's, the phone rang. My dad called and requested that one of us go pick up our cousin from the police station.

My sisters and I had no idea we had this cousin! Confused by the backstory of my dad's brother and a woman we had never met, we pieced together that there was an almost four-month-old baby boy with our DNA, and if we didn't go pick him up, he would be placed into the child welfare system.

Though I didn't know I had this cousin, I did know all about the child welfare system. I had been working at a non-profit alcohol and drug treatment facility in Cleveland and knew that a mother had twenty-two months to complete the goals of her case plan and reunite with her child after a removal. I knew that addiction is a disease that requires treatment. I knew the terms *kinship care, foster care*, and *adoption*. I didn't know that God had prepared me for a time such as this.

Most people, whether they plan on having a child or are surprised by the announcement, have nine months to mentally, physically, and emotionally prepare. At twenty-seven, I was not ill-prepared to be a mom, and it was definitely something I always wanted to be. But that Christmas I was not expecting or prepared to receive the gift of a child—a beautiful bundle of joy!

The moment the officer handed him to me, I felt it. The moment the baby's eyes met mine, the feeling I had just hours before from the boy at Denny's came over me again, and tears streamed down my face. I saw God in his eyes. God was asking us, "Are you ready to be selfless? Are you ready to love a child and to put your needs aside? Are you ready to grow up?"

We, without hesitation, said, "Yes, we are!" We brought Vinny home.

Moments that change us can be crude, harsh moments, but they can also be these jaw-dropping, awe-inspiring, overwhelming, unexplainable moments of love. Watching this baby sleeping in a car seat on our living room floor, because we had no crib, a thought paralyzed me. I questioned my worthiness to hold one of God's greatest gifts, a child, unborn to me but in my care and responsibility. I could not take my eyes off him. I was in love. I was in awe. I was a mom.

The details of the next fourteen months are a blur as visits from social workers, parenting classes, and juggling work and child care coincided with wedding planning. We had become a family in a moment. I can honestly say that this time in my life was equally charged, both positive and negative. It was as if all things were falling into place, yet I was scared that they were falling at all. God's plan had never disappointed me, and I needed to continue that trust as the thought of getting close to this child, then having to send him home, haunted me. I was scared. Scared to love him. Scared to lose him. Scared to have him call me mom, but what else should he call the person who loves him as if he were her own?

People read or hear stories and say, "I would have done..." or "Why didn't...," but the fact is no one knows what he or she will do in a given moment until that moment is presented. The thought of becoming a mother is exciting for some and terrifying for others. I didn't have time to think. No second thought was given. This child needed me. I needed him. It was God's plan.

But *was* it God's plan for him to stay with me? I had not thought about what would happen next. I hadn't given a thought to how this would end. He had a mother. She was trying to get better. I wanted her to get better for him. She had twenty-two months to do that. Could I be his mother for twenty-two months and then just stop?

Of course, I wanted her to get well. I know what addictions can do, and I don't wish that on anyone. Ironically, she was receiving treatment from some of the best—the facility where I worked. While I was caring for her child, she was attending groups. I could see her if I wanted to, but I didn't. I focused on Vinny, keeping him safe and mothering him the best way I knew how without being his mom.

Immediately, Vinny and I bonded. Without a doubt, I was a mom, his mom. He was my priority. My heart beamed for him. My schedule revolved around him. Vinny's dad's acceptance and love for him as if he was his own son is the most selfless act I've seen firsthand. And in February of 2005, we were thrilled to find out that I was pregnant and that we would be parents in October. Our existence as individuals and as a couple had a definable purpose—to care for these children.

I had to prepare myself for so many things—being pregnant for the first time, giving birth to a child, and feeling the emptiness without Vinny. I tried but couldn't consider my life without him. Comfort came by remembering I was blessed to be having a child of my own. Peace came from knowing that he is my cousin—so he would always be in my life, right? But could I stop being his mom? Could I love him as much as I would love my own children? Could I love my own children as much as I loved Vinny? Could I trust that he would be safe with them?

During these moments, I had to trust God's plan and come to an understanding that God and Vinny needed me, even if only temporarily. I had to trust that this woman, whom I didn't know and who didn't know me, would have the same compassion and love that we did! I had to trust that she would allow us to be a part of his life. I had to trust that I could handle whatever God intended.

I knew it was going to be hard. I just didn't know how hard. Pregnant for the first time, my emotions were heightened. My maternal instincts were on fire within me, and I needed, we needed, this child needed to know his fate. He needed to know whom to call Mom! Giving birth to a child is an act; mothering a child is a gift. Not everyone who gives birth can or should parent, and not every parent needs to birth a child. This child was not mine, but that moment God trusted his life to me, I became his mom. I was confounded by the extent of my love for someone.

That love gave me the strength and courage to pick up the phone and have a very difficult conversation with my uncle, one in which I asked him and his wife to consider relinquishing custody of their son to me. Asking was hard, but wondering how it would make them feel was harder. It was a risk, for sure, as they could have easily taken offense and never let me see him again. What were the chances they would agree that it was in Vinny's best interest for him to build a home with me and call me Mom, as three more boys would eventually do.

July 6, 2005	Vinny's Moment
October 28, 2005	David's Moment
June 21, 2008	Nathaniel's Moment
March 28, 2012	Noah's Moment

In Vinny's moment, he legally became ours. That little secret from Denny's wasn't a secret for long. I couldn't, and still can't, tell Vinny's story without starting with that. It was the moment I saw God. It was the day He sent his only son to Earth and the day He gave me mine. It is my God-given honor, privilege, and lifelong responsibility to be Vinny's, David's, Nathaniel's, and Noah's mom, whose births were all unique and amazing moments that made me not just a mom, but who I am as a person. Though we officially celebrate their birthdays, every moment I have with them is celebrated!

Watching my boys become who God intended takes a continued trust. When I get anxious or worried, I remember that His plan prevails and that I can look into their eyes and see Him. It gives me peace. Each time I found out I was pregnant, I would question if I could love this one as much as I loved the others. The answer was always yes! It doesn't matter how many children you have, you can love them all—and that is exactly what God does! He loves us all.

The moment I held Vinny was the moment I learned that a mom isn't the person who gives you life. A mom is the one who guides you to it and through it. My mom has been there for me for all the moments that have changed me so far. She is the one who guides me to it and through it. I learned about being a mom from the best.

It is also my God-given honor, privilege, and lifelong responsibility to be a daughter, a sister, a friend, and the best human I can be. God doesn't make mistakes. Had my dad not called that night, I would not have been a mom to Vinny. My dad knew the situation was complicated, and he knew I could get hurt. He knew that parenting was hard and tried to protect me. He was right. The situation was complicated, hard, and painful, but what I've come to realize is that it wasn't the situation that was all of those things; it was life, and it still is.

Being human requires a level of trust difficult to conceive and harder to maintain. Vinny opened my eyes to that trust, and it remains with me as I attempt to teach it to my boys. But they will need their own complicated, hard and painful moments, their crude and harsh moments, their jaw-dropping, awe-inspiring, overwhelming, and unexplainable moments of love to find it.

February 4, 2018

My dad was diagnosed with pancreatic cancer on June 21, 2017. That was a crude, harsh moment, but we rallied, and he decided he wanted to stay as active and well as long as he could without going through treatments. We knew the time would come, regardless, but agreed that we could do some great things and make the most of the time we had.

We had just completed an amazing cruise through Europe. We planned train rides and concerts like Queen and Billy Joel. We had a wonderful holiday season with him, which is when he gave up the diet and enjoyed his final days the best he could.

The moment came on Super Bowl Sunday. None of us thought that would be the day. No one expected it to be the moment it happened. He grabbed our hands and said his final words, "Hail, Mary," as we held hands around him and finished the prayer. I stared into his eyes, once again seeing God. As his eyes focused on the ceiling, clearly seeing something I couldn't, I watched the light leave his eyes. His body stayed with us another four hours, but he wasn't there anymore. His soul had returned home.

I was as unprepared for my dad's passing as I was for becoming a mother. I wanted more time to become emotionally, mentally, and physically ready for both. I realized in that moment that you can't prepare for the moments that change you, no matter how hard you try. You just have to have faith and trust that it is part of His plan. That, my friend, is every moment's secret.

"

We are made for moments
that make us, even if those
moments belong to someone
else. Feel them. Grow with
them. Allow them to change
you for the better.

"

4

Her Fight

Scarlett Green-Wright and Natalie Zangara Friedl

September 12, 2022

My baby girl.

I can't breathe.

I can't sleep.

A mother's worst nightmare, they call it. It's NOT! I can wake up from a nightmare, and my daughter is whole...well, speaking, walking, present. This is NOT a nightmare. This is tragic reality. It feels fake. I feel numb. Nothing is familiar.

Nothing was unusual. I checked her location, and she was on her way to me. We proceeded to build her homecoming float. With each addition, each decoration, I knew she would be more thrilled. She is on the homecoming court. She is a basketball star. She is college-bound. She is on her way.

I had protected her. I had guided her. I had done everything within my control to ensure her future. Our excitement about her future was uncontrollable, and we thought we had everything under control. I didn't realize how little control we had. I didn't know she had lost control of her vehicle. That moment was beyond our control.

When the call comes through that your child has been in an accident, you have trained yourself to NOT expect the worst. The worst fleetingly crosses your mind, but you have sixteen years telling you that she has always been okay, except for maybe a broken bone, a scratch, a bump because accidents happen. A child gets hurt, a child heals, and we say, "That could have been worse," and "Thank God it wasn't!"

The worst is what we endured. A single-car accident off the exit ramp of that Houston highway. Yet, still, she is going to be okay! Right? We could see the mangled car off in the distance. We could hear the Life Flight transport above our heads. I had not seen her. I did not need to. I felt her. Then,

I fell to my knees…I think? I don't remember exactly. I don't want to. You wouldn't either.

* * * * *

Only once since the accident, as I write this with her, has Scarlett, Zoe's mom, been past the site of the accident. The sight is too much for a mother. Writing this is too much for a mother. But it needs to be written because never is a moment in time so changing, so altering that neither of these words seem enough to describe it. The moment became the flip from *before* to *after*. The people, places, and things seem familiar, but when you see your baby helpless and clinging to this world, you are not the same. Nothing is.

Circular thoughts interrupted by stabbing pains of shock that last for days. Hanging on to every last bit of hope, as if drinking the last drop of water without any knowledge of where the next drop will come from…over and over again. Comfort is absent. Hugs are just pressure, and smiles make her wonder if she will ever see Zoe's again.

Yet she needed all of them. She needed the hugs. She needed the smiles. She needed the prayers. She would not call herself religious, but definitely spiritual; she needed something and He gave it to her. He gave her the ever-widening circle of energy and prayer to ease just enough of the pain so she could watch the sun set and rise again the next day, never knowing if it would be her daughter's last.

Doctors, from their best perspectives, would speculate as to Zoe's prognosis. There was no speculating about the severity of the impact she had endured as she struck the front window and was thrown through the rear window. Statistics tell us that 75 percent of people die on impact. The statistics don't tell us how many of the 25 percent who live go back to being who they were before an accident. Because no one does. Not Zoe. Not Scarlett. Not Zoe's Tribe, Scarlett's besties from high school. The daily text thread of prayers, broken-heart emojis, and questions we ask without actually wanting to know the answers to. We would wonder and weaken with every response that shared the details of the accident. Imagining—but just can't imagine—how Scarlett is still breathing…still sleeping. It is only because He is in control that she is doing those things.

* * * * *

Her daughter was not moving. Her daughter was not speaking. For over two weeks, she watched the lifeless body and thanked God for being in control of Zoe's breath and heart-beat—her only signs of life. Scarlett moved. Scarlett talked. She had no choice. Her involuntary movements continued as she only wanted to lie motionless next to her daughter. She wanted the world to stop too. She wanted it all to STOP, but was also so afraid that it might. The slow and debilitating realization that her daughter is present, but without promise of ever being whole, creates a time warp of the longest hours and the shortest days.

* * * * *

Take a moment and imagine. It will change you as well, at least temporarily. Just like those movies you watch that stay with you long after the end credits, but over time, the impact fades. You go back to being the same. When it is reality, then physically, spiritually, emotionally, and in a realm of no understanding, you are changed. The hours become days, the days become weeks, and the weeks, months. As we write this, we are just over four months in. As you read this, it may be years later, but it doesn't matter because that moment will never change, regardless of how much time passes. We know you can feel it. You are meant to feel it.

Overwhelmed with support, with love, with prayers, with cards and gifts, with sympathy and tears. Those days were surreal. Scarlett learned more about Zoe than she ever knew before, like her ability to withstand surgery after surgery. She witnessed her strength and her resilience to trauma. She saw the physical alterations of her daughter's appearance drastically contradicting the photos she sent as prayer updates.

Thousands of faces dampened with tears over the first two months as this story unfolded. Love and support for Zoe and for her passenger, who went almost physically unharmed, but certainly emotionally scarred, poured out. He was released from the hospital the evening of the accident. He has answers to questions that the family will never ask because asking doesn't change reality. Zoe's moment was felt by the whole community, then the city, the state, and the nation. Raising awareness and funds for the family, the community came out to show their love and support for this young girl.

Why? Because of who she is! She is kind, generous, compassionate, and loving. She would have been the first to rush to see how she could help, the first to donate, and the first to make sure the community wrapped around someone in need. Zoe's Tribe, from Boston, Detroit, Columbus, Cleveland, Cincinnati, and Houston, and all across the country, focus on what needs done, like prayers, meals, financial support and love. Even today, prayer is key and #prayforzoe on Facebook highlights the timeline of her journey and the communication from the hospital bed to the world that loves her.

Support is constant. Photos on #sunsetsforzoe are shared from all over the country and the world, so she can catch glimpses of the ones she has missed; #flowersforzoe posts brighten her room with encouraging messages and beautiful art. Sweatshirts are made with Zoe's artwork shared by her

African American studies teacher and are worn by friends and strangers alike. But the outpouring of support continues to this day, with no sign of ceasing. This incredible love exists because we all realize the same thing—it could be any one of us, and no one wants anyone to endure this raw, unceasing pain.

* * * * *

Driving to and from the hospital, with the movie of the moment constantly running in her mind, contributes to Scarlett's exhaustion. And as the adrenaline wears off and time begins to slow down, what is left is the shift from denial and anger to acceptance and hope. When you allow yourself to feel all there is to feel, to ask for and receive the support that surrounds you, and to lean on your Creator, your Healer, your Miracle Worker, the moment that changed you becomes painfully beautiful.

Every time her friends visit, I see a Facebook memo, watch an old TikTok of her, or walk into this hospital room, it's like a crushing force on my chest, a constant reminder of everything she is no longer and of the daughter I have lost. It's a constant grieving process that never gets better. Zoe and I did everything together. The bond we have is unlike anything I've ever known. Every day, my heart is literally aching. I don't know why this had to happen to her...to me...to our family. I'm just so sad. I just want Zoe back. I have been so busy focusing on the next thing—surgery, transfer, appointments, milestones — that I haven't sat for any given time with my grief. She is my firstborn, my baby girl. She is my... my whole world.

This doesn't, this can't, capture the pain that exists in a mother's heart. But you feel it. You aren't meant to be the same after the moment your story changes, but other's stories, when truly shared and felt, can have the same effect. Why is that important? Because we are made to feel and grow and give. We are made for moments that make us, even if those moments belong to someone else. Feel them. Grow with them. Allow them to change you for the better.

To go to it and through it—the pain, grief, confusion, anxiety—is the ultimate challenge. We cannot ignore it. We can't numb it. We can't go around it. It will find us. It will haunt us. It will debilitate us if we do not allow ourselves the time and space to walk through it, eyes wide open, no substances, and no filter to curb its impact. Just raw, breathtaking pain. It feels as if it could kill you, but it's changing you. And the parts of you that have changed have experienced a sort of death. Pure love and connection allows us to feel this. To protect ourselves from this pain would be to rob ourselves of love. The other side of feeling empty is to feel complete, and this cannot happen without love. It is that love, that connection, that weakens our knees at even the thought of loss. And, of course, the pain is worth it because the love is so great.

* * * * *

December 14, 2022

Scarlett waits. Every day, the family waits and wonders if Zoe will ever be the same. If anything will ever be the same, and the answer is no. Her journey will continue to change all of us.

One month in a coma in the Shock Trauma ICU, unable to communicate, not following commands, no meaningful movement, and had only opened her eyes a few times. Two months in TIRR Memorial Hermann Disorders of Consciousness Program, which focuses on patients in a vegetative or minimally conscious state, allowed Zoe to come home. After twelve surgeries, multiple ankle casts, a tracheotomy, a craniotomy, and a feeding tube, she can communicate, hold her head up straight, and stand with help; she's working every day to get stronger and walk again. Praise God! I have seen God work His miracle on Zoe, and I know He is not done yet.

What happens next, day in and day out, as Zoe heals and as the family embraces this new reality, will continue to be painfully beautiful, like all of our lives. Empathy and compassion allow us to love. To feel what others may be feeling, if even only for an instant, is a gift and a curse. We go through our days wishing others could experience the world from our perspective, instead of putting blinders on to the experiences of others. Shared moments like these bring us closer to human actualization, the realization or fulfillment of the potentialities of humans.

Zoe's gift to you is this moment when you can become better than you were before you read this. The moments that change us happen every second, yet so often we choose to stay the same. Comfortable. Safe. Normal. How great could we be for each other if we allowed ourselves to feel, to go "to it and through it" and then help others to do the same?

Moments that change us are not generally subtle and soft. The crude and harsh moments that change us in an instant are not planned. They are not easily accepted. They are lasting and vast in their impact. Accidents happen, but this, Zoe's accident, was no accident. It was a part of her journey. It expedited who and how she will impact this Earth and the people in it—Scarlett, her family and friends, and, now, each of you.

We know Zoe's story could have ended much differently, and so can yours. Her second chance at life was for all of us. We hope it's not like a movie, its impact fading with time. We hope that this story is a crude and harsh moment for you so that you love bigger and harder than you ever have before. Zoe's understanding of what happened that day will be a process. The important things—like her zest for life, her spunky attitude, her love of others, and her beautiful smile—are even bigger than they were before. They will go with her into her future. She will share them with the world, regardless of the moment that changed her. Zoe will tell you for herself one day, but for now, and right now, see the sunset for all that it is, and let that light shine within you each morning you are given breath. There are no endings to these moments, just impacts. Her story, this story, is just beginning. Her fight is our fight.

"

Discover your flight, just
as a caterpillar sheds its
cocoon in order to transform
into a butterfly. Trust and
have faith in your intuition.

"

5

Learning to Fly

Crista Salvatore

"Crista, if you don't quit tomorrow, you will have a nervous breakdown."

Those words from my therapist terrified me because it was my truth. I knew in the depth of my soul that I needed to leave my job, which meant letting go of the fancy title, the benefits, and the regular paycheck. The conundrum was that I was in no position to leave. I lived alone in one of the most expensive places in the world, a one-bedroom apartment I loved in the Upper East Side in Manhattan, and didn't want to move. I had no partner or roommate to help pay the bills.

From the first interview with Jane, I suspected the working relationship with my boss may not be the best fit. There were more signs along the way, but I didn't listen. I ignored the whispers within and cast them aside. I could no longer deny the whispers when they turned into consequences. The consequences took a front-row seat in my life, and I was losing myself. The job hijacked my mental, spiritual, emotional, and physical well-being.

The physical impact was the most concerning. I was not sleeping, my eye started twitching, and I had constant headaches. Our bodies are constantly communicating with us; I finally listened to mine and booked an appointment at NYU for an MRI of my head. I was scared. It was a blessing that the scan showed there were no abnormalities.

It became crystal clear, after the first six months on the job, I was screwed. I worked for a perfectionist. I knew the type because I was a recovering perfectionist myself. Jane asked me to redo decks at least five times over—change the color on the graphic, adjust the font size, rewrite a sentence, and so on. Nothing was ever good enough, and the constant nit-picking was exhausting. I was getting paid a lot of money to make those minor, inconsequential adjustments. It was ridiculous and soul sucking. That way of working was not sustainable. It took time away from using my gift, which was connecting and supporting leaders. I had no power, even though I had the fancy title of senior director and made the most money I ever had in my life. Interestingly, you would think that as I went higher up in the organization, I would have a voice. Not the case here. Let's face it; no one wants to be micromanaged. I felt so stifled that I couldn't breathe.

About eight months into the role, I spoke up, and senior leadership assigned me to a new manager, Andrew. I thought that change would be the answer to my prayers. Shortly after, I realized that it was too late; I had stayed too long in the abuse. At that point, my anxiety was at an all-time high. I was unhinged. I was no longer productive and was unable to perform my job successfully. How could I help leaders grow when I was empty? I had nothing to give to myself, let alone others. But instead of leaving that month, I stayed. I didn't want LinkedIn to show that I held that job for only seven months, and I didn't want to give back my signing bonus. I realize now that I consistently betrayed myself by not honoring my needs and respecting my boundaries.

Which brings me to the come-to-Jesus meeting with my therapist a few months later. That conversation about my being on the verge of breakdown gave me the jolt I needed to act. The next day, I gave my new boss a resignation letter, along with a bottle of wine for the holidays. At the time it seemed the polite thing to do, but it definitely sent mixed messages. I was split as well; part of me felt bad about leaving, as if I were a total failure for only lasting fifteen months in the job. The other part of me was relieved. Unfortunately, my boss's reaction was far from compassionate or even understanding. He said I was making a big mistake and an impulsive decision. He was wrong, though; the hard truth was I should have quit after the first six months. Andrew was more concerned about his ego and reputation. But it really did not matter what he thought or what he said. I needed to choose me, no matter what the consequences were. The healthiest way out was to exit somewhat gracefully and focus on putting myself back together physically and emotionally. When I walked through those doors for the last time, I felt free and never looked back.

The first month, I felt liberated. It was a relief not having to go back to my small cube in an office on Park Avenue. I went on a trip to Tulum, which I had already planned with a friend, and from there flew to Florida to visit my parents. As I approached the end of my time in Florida, I fell sick with bronchitis. The anxiety was building, getting stronger and stronger as I faced the reality around the corner. The initial relief was now a distant feeling. I always say, "The body doesn't lie." It is constantly speaking to you, whether you listen to it or not. When we ignore the signals, it comes alive with a vengeance. There's no escaping it.

I was faced with figuring out what was next. I didn't realize that the real discomfort, pain, and struggle had just begun. Questions were swirling in my mind. *What am I to do now? Will I survive?* These all hit deep, and I felt real uncertainty. I was back to not sleeping and feeling trapped once again.

For a couple of weeks, every minute felt like an eternity. It was almost as though I existed in a cocoon. I had no desire to see anyone, and I stayed in my 850-square-foot apartment.

I had no appetite, which was incredibly strange because I am a person who loves food; that was one of the main reasons I appreciated living in NYC. Half of the charges on my credit card statement were related to food. In the past, I had definitely indulged by eating at some fabulous restaurants.

My parents were very concerned; they did not know what to do to help me. And I had no clue myself. I was so lost. They said to buy a ticket and come to Florida, but that meant I had to leave my apartment and deal with people. Both those tasks were daunting, even though generally I was an extrovert who liked connecting with people. There were days that I was lucky just to muster enough energy to walk around the block.

One especially dark week, I thought I may need to be committed—go away somewhere for a month. A close friend found a psychiatrist for me who was only one block away from my apartment. I swear that resource was a gift from God because, at the time, my regular therapist was out of the country due to a family tragedy. I took meds for a day or two and then put them aside. I remember the psychiatrist explaining the dilemma of taking medications. It can be difficult to treat anxious people, especially when it comes to prescribing medication. They feel anxiety when they take meds, and they feel anxious when they don't. It is a no-win scenario. I really got that and felt it. I now fully understand why some people take meds to function. Through that painful time, I developed much more empathy and compassion for those who are struggling with mental illness.

I had heard these periods of life being referred to as the "dark night of the soul." They occur when a person undergoes a difficult and significant transition to a deeper meaning of life and then questions their place in it. Everything they have known feels uncomfortable. This heightened awareness is accompanied by a painful shedding of identity, relationships, career, and belief systems that previously allowed them to construct significance in their life. This is what happened to me. It was hell. I was no longer comfortable in my own skin, and my life no longer aligned with my soul.

How could I get back to me? No clue. I felt I had a high level of consciousness, so why was this happening to me? How could I become me once again? It is almost as though I had to create an entirely new foundation for myself. It is easy to give advice to others and offer up solutions, but it is much more challenging when you have to confront yourself. With all the therapy, self-help books, and personal-development seminars I'd paid for, you'd think I'd have it all figured out. However, I was back to square one, and the only thing I knew to do was ask God for help. I felt that faith was the only thing that was going to make me whole and sane again.

The good news was that I had some savings from a condo sale and all the time in the world. But I was also terrified at the prospect of using that time to confront my fears and anxiety. There were no distractions. It was a gift that I had that money for therapy, rent, and daily living expenses, so I invested in me. After two years, I had gone through all my savings and then some, but it was what I had to do to get to a healthy place. I had to figure out who I was and how to align myself with what my soul was telling me: change my trajectory, change my path.

Yet I still didn't make a change that first year; I went back to what I thought was the safe option, looking for full-time employment, even though I wasn't emotionally or physically ready. I was disinterested in getting the same type of full-time HR position, but I looked anyway. I associated security with working for a corporation. It is interesting how it was not happening for me; even the jobs I thought I wanted would suddenly change or no longer be available. Through the process of interviewing, I was putting my energy and effort into securing another situation in which I did not belong. Yet again, I wasn't aware of or listening to what the world was telling me. As a result, I was left discouraged and frustrated.

At first, I loved not having to go anywhere, but then it became uncomfortable. I felt that I had no purpose, no direction. I realized that I needed to use my skills again for good, to create structure in my life. I decided to volunteer at a women's shelter, and it was one of the best decisions I've ever made. It was a mirror for me. In ways, I was the same as the women I was serving. I was a mentor, there to encourage and support women in moving forward. I felt my coaching would help them follow their passions. The bigger their dream, the better; I functioned as their coach and was never one to squash anyone's hopes and aspirations. Even though I was supposed to be the expert, I was no better than they.

It was a reality check, forcing me to accept where I was. Just like the women in the shelter, I was starting over and rebuilding. We were all trying to come out of the dark and find our own way. I was humbled and grateful for the experience. When the women took the mentoring very seriously, it made me feel that I was worthy and that someone believed in what I had to offer, even though at the time I was struggling and feeling insignificant. Showing up on Thursday nights gave me purpose, which was a true gift. My hope is that the mentoring was as meaningful for them as it was for me.

I'd like to say that everything fell into place, that a year later everything had worked itself out, and that it only took a little time for my life to become all sunshine and rainbows. But that definitely was not the case. It was a marathon, not a sprint. Do I wish that I had embraced the changes a bit faster, learned the lessons earlier? Yes, sometimes. That's not how my life unfolded, though. My healing came in my own divine timing and with the prayers and support from my family and friends along the way. As I started to honor my cadence, listen to my own voice, and align my actions with my values, my life slowly transformed. I was shedding the day-to-day routine that I was accustomed to, which no longer worked for me, even though I had no clue what was next. I learned to respect the relationship I had with myself—discovering and communicating my limits, listening to my body, acknowledging my emotions, and making space for my needs.

Almost seven years later, my life looks completely different. I am learning to lean in and love all parts of me—the six-year-old, the fear, the anger, the creativity, my big heart, and the resiliency. I now run my own business, which is a more abundant life, and I live on my terms. There's an element of freedom I created for myself that has impacted my presence in the world. It has been such a different way of working. I am incredibly grateful for my clients and the projects that come my way. I thought I needed to have others create security and stability for me, but I uncovered that the ability was always within me. Now I listen to the whispers, even when I don't want to acknowledge them. I know they are serving me, and when I am fully inspired, I am able to use my gifts from God.

What brought you to my story? I feel you are reading this for a reason. Is there something you need to let go? How will you learn to fly?

My hope is you discover your flight, just as a caterpillar sheds its cocoon in order to transform into a butterfly. Trust and have faith in your intuition. Only God and you know the truth and the path to fulfilling your destiny here on Earth. Be fearless and listen.

"

You're alive. Act like it. Call
a friend, or go to the gym, or
do things that people who are
truly alive do.

"

6

Stumbling into Growth

Cammie Smith

As I'm sitting at my computer and writing this, I have spent about 7,660 days alive. I've only spent about 182 days truly living.

Let me give you some background. About 182 days ago, my life changed over something as silly as a staircase.

That staircase caused a Flight For Life, medical paralysis, two months in and out of the hospital, three brain injuries, and the desperate need for a shoulder replacement. The

EMTs shook their heads when people asked how I was doing. Doctors didn't know what survival looked like, and if I would walk again due to paralysis, or talk again due to how hard I hit my head. The brain injuries were predicted to have caused permanent cognitive damage in the right side of my brain, the part of the brain that controls memory, attention, reasoning, and problem-solving skills. All pretty important things.

One of the few days that I remember from the early stages of my injury was the day that I woke up and started talking. Shortly after, I started walking. Thereafter, I began dancing around my hospital room, against all medical odds, while eating the best chocolate chip cookies my mom DoorDashed to me every day. I danced despite the black eyes, shoulder sling, and the obvious cognitive issues. I was so happy. I felt this overwhelming amount of joy for life.

I was also in a lot of denial. Although my recovery made me "a walking, talking miracle," according to my doctors, my recovery process had just started.

My two months in and out of the hospital were two of the hardest months on record for me. That's not saying much—being a twenty-year-old girl, I've barely lived—but I hope it will never be topped. Throughout my time in the hospital I had to reteach myself basic daily functions, which was the biggest slice of humble pie ever. I learned how to walk in a straight line and balance on one foot again. I was asked to read paragraph-long stories and then tell my therapist what I remembered. After reading each one aloud, I looked up and had no idea what I'd just read. Almost daily, I had to match color names to the correct colors on this stupid color-blocked pad—I was awful at it. I hated it. Nearly every therapy session, when the word *red* popped up on the computer screen, I clicked the yellow square. I did this every time without fail.

One day I just looked at my therapist and started crying. Crying due to frustration, anger, and confusion as to why I couldn't comprehend the simple task and click a red square. Identifying the color red is something a toddler can do. My therapist took me to get ice cream after that. It was the worst hospital ice cream ever, but the gesture was sweet.

The day after my color meltdown, something clicked in my head, and I got it right. I clicked the red square when the word *red* came on the computer. I cried tears of JOY this time, feeling like the strongest person on the face of the planet. According to all of my therapists and doctors, a smile never left my face for my remaining time in the hospital.

I feel I had every right to be mad at the world. I'm a full-time college student who is in a sorority and loves being around people. Learning that I wasn't allowed to go back to college, not to mention realizing that I didn't have the neurological capability to participate in academics, was tough. Then I was told that I had to spend the next five months at home, that I needed surgery, and that I couldn't drive, ski, or read. And according to the doctor's orders, I couldn't even be left alone. I felt as if this were close to the end of the world for me. My world got flipped upside down.

It wasn't all bad though. I learned how to control my anger and apologize when I was in the wrong. Apparently brain injuries can cause you to have outbursts of aggression. My mom received the brunt of that, unfortunately. I also learned how to deal with my recovery and use the help I was given to the fullest extent.

Since my accident, I feel the happiest and most mentally stable I ever have in my life. Colors are brighter; I laugh harder and love more. People ask how I'm so happy, given my situation, and I think I figured it out. We have no control over what happens to us on a day-to-day basis. Some of it can be seriously fucked up and life altering, or it can be as innocuous as rain when you wanted sunshine. It's still out of our control. I couldn't control that I fell down a staircase, and I refuse to live in fear of them for the rest of my life. Usually a staircase isn't something people are afraid of—why should they be?

I could've blamed everything on my accident, from 182 days ago forward. But I didn't. Instead, I took control of my life. I controlled my thankfulness for the people surrounding me who supported me unconditionally. I controlled how thankful I was that I didn't die and that I could still walk and talk. I controlled my learning from, and listening to, all of my therapists in the hospital, no matter how much I didn't want to. I controlled how hard I worked in my six-hour, daily therapy sessions. I controlled never taking no for an answer from anyone if it was something I wholeheartedly believed in.

I constantly ask myself a lot of questions. Why did I get a second chance? Why did I get to live when people with my same exact injuries didn't? Why did I have the strength to say, "I'm not done on this Earth yet"? Why did I defy every single assumption about my recovery?

I don't think I will ever know why. It's one of the many mysteries of the world I will never figure out. I have come to terms with that and am okay with it. Maybe one day I'll give someone a hug when they need it; maybe I will change the world. Maybe one day it will just click, and I will figure out the answer. But I know I'm here for a reason; that is also true for each of you readers. For now, all I can do with the life that's been given back to me is to live it for the people who can't.

I love for people who can't love. I run, walk, and jump for all the people who no longer have the ability to do so. I use my mind and move my body because I have the ability to distinguish red and yellow and balance on one foot again. I put my efforts into school or work for all the people who no longer have the cognitive abilities to do so.

You're alive. Act like it. Call a friend, or go to the gym, or do things that people who are truly alive do. I do all of these because I was so close to being one of the people who can't.

This frame of time has been easily the craziest part of my young adult life. I have never experienced so many different emotions at one time. Through this, I became a better sister, friend, daughter, student, and all the roles I continue to hold. I learned so much about myself and the world surrounding me. Some of my key takeaways:

You will end up where you are supposed to be. Rejection is redirection, and everything happens for a reason. If you haven't found that reason, it's not over yet. And that's okay. Growth is the most uncomfortable feeling ever. It's uncomfortable because you have never been there before. And that's also okay. Fight hard for what you believe in and what you think is right. Never take no for an answer; keep pushing. True love won't allow alternatives. When it's right, it's impossible to walk away. Love people as you love the oxygen you breathe.

It's not your job to figure out why someone does or does not see your value. Whatever you may be going through, never compare it to someone else's pain. There's no scale; pain is different for everyone. Never devalue what others are going through. Listen to other people's sides of stories you thought you knew everything about. Make sure you hug your mom, dad, and loved ones while you still can. Smile at strangers because you never know who needs it. Do everything in your power to be who you are and who you want to be, because only you can control your actions. You control your own happiness, how you feel, and your outlook on life. Try to find the thing you would die for. Then start living for that purpose.

As for me, I learned I am exactly where I need to be.

> I knew it was time to seek out the glitter that dusts even the most ordinary of circumstances.

7

Hope Glitters

Sabrina VanDine Smith

There was a quiet moment when the world shifted for me. A moment no one else would notice, not even me, until several months later. But it was the moment I found my strength again.

I struggle with the notion that everything happens for a reason. But what I've been exploring lately is just a small pivot: everything **prepares** you for a reason.

In 2018 I started to lose my balance. And by losing my balance I mean I would be walking straight down the hall and my right leg would kick out to the side as if controlled by someone else's brain. Then came the double vision and general confusion. By the time I checked myself into the hospital, I was walking bent over at a 90-degree angle (without noticing) and hallucinating. And by hallucinating I mean I told the doctors that not only were my children on their way to see me for visiting hours, but to do so they were being deflated and transported through the electrical outlet, only to reinflate once they arrived to spend time with me.

Autoimmune encephalitis. I won't bore you with the details. But essentially my immune system decided to light my brain on fire. And, I'm told, it was up to the doctors to (a) put out the fire and then (b) heal the burned damage.

I have flashes of my month in the hospital: voices screaming on the neurological floor, an occupational therapist who was so hard on me I credit her for saving my life (I called her Connie instead of Trisha, and to this day I can't remember why), a service dog they brought by to cheer up patients, and an attempt to sneak to the bathroom in the middle of the night, which resulted in setting off my bed alarm. I only really remember the last four days. We now, with a bit of time behind us, jokingly call it my March Madness.

Fun fact: After twenty-eight days in the hospital, I was still hallucinating the day I was discharged. I think that I felt I was healed, but at a certain point hospital psychosis becomes real, and I so desperately wanted to be home. There was a full-blown party of imaginary people in my room the morning my doctor came in to discharge me, which I just didn't mention to him. I never had another hallucination after that day.

Recovery was brutal. My first day of in-home therapy, I was asked to name in a minute as many words as possible that started with the letter *C*. I could name one. *Cup.* There was a glass of water right in front of me as a big hint. Learning to think and building up strength to walk again is nothing if not humbling. The first few days home, my husband, Doug, had to put a leash on me to walk me up the stairs. He also had to listen to my cognitive therapist try and get me to remember a simple repetition of three words. And to select which picture was a rhinoceros and which was an elephant.

With three months of recovery and a clean bill of health behind me, I remember rounding the corner into 2020 and thinking how on Earth was I going to make it through March, remembering all the anniversary milestones of my illness as they came and went—the day I entered the hospital, the day I left, each day that I had my husband note on my hospital calendar so I wouldn't forget and have to keep asking him.

Then Covid happened—we called it Corona then—and the world changed. We didn't know what we didn't know. And so I missed visits with my parents, afraid I would bring the virus with me.

My dad was becoming ill and delayed medical care as this was around the time "they" were telling people to cancel medical appointments unless absolutely necessary. I often wonder, when the news is screaming about inflated numbers of Covid deaths, should the question be how many deaths are attributable to Covid due to people missing doctor's appointments and not taking care of their general health.

My dad was checked into the hospital, and while he was in the hospital, my mom checked herself in for a cough as well. A day later she was on a ventilator.

When I got the call to get on a plane, that my dad was dying, there were protocols in place in California that stated you were only allowed in a hospital if your family member was dying. I arrived as my dad was in a state of "actively dying." Because my mom was on a ventilator three doors down, the nurses turned their backs and let my brother and me visit her as well.

I'll never forget those kind nurses, who were supposed to only allow us one visit, gathering together as I overheard one say, "I'm not going to be the one to kick those kids out." (Kids who were fifty and forty-seven at the time and were about to become orphans.) She let us leave and come back three times while she pretended not to notice.

My dad's death was nothing short of beautiful. My brother was so incredibly strong. He played my dad's favorite songs

(Billy Joel's "Still Rock and Roll to Me"), showed him endless pictures on his tablet, and told a multitude of stories so my dad would hear my brother's voice, all while I fell apart. I've always been the strong daughter, but my brother... My brother absolutely shone. Upon reflection, I often wonder if my dad's strength was somehow transferred to my brother at that moment.

We had Last Rites performed (over the phone because of the pandemic) and told my unconscious mom on our way out the door that our dad was gone.

My mom eventually recovered, and we had six bonus months with her. But she became ill again and was admitted back into the hospital. By then, Covid protocols had eased a bit, but not completely. I was told to "save" my visit for when she was doing better. They put her back on a ventilator and then had to perform a "routine" surgery.

She died alone, no family with her. As beautiful as our dad's passing was, I feel our mom was cheated. Her last words to the doctor before she was placed on the ventilator were, "I don't want to die; I have too much to do." I live with that every day. I struggled with including this detail, but it's part of my healing. And my growth. And her story. Somehow I feel we tried to make up for this moment by getting a special dispensation from the Catholic Church to have "The Dance" by Garth Brooks played at her funeral. Something she had told us she wanted from the time we were little.

Two things you have to know about my parents—they were so much a part of my life, and they were larger than life. Were they flawed? Of course. But they were the absolute best. My childhood was just about as perfect as it could be. My dad taught me my work ethic and how to take a compliment, and my mom taught me that life is a theme party, so you may as well dress up. And they both taught me to be kind, realistic, and not take myself too seriously. And uplighting—my parents would say uplighting makes a home.

Having a double funeral for your parents is something I hope no one has to do, but my brother and I did. And once again my brother was a total rock star and handled every little detail. While I was having trouble regaining my footing, he was building slide shows, choosing a menu they would both love, and making sure to call our parents' friends personally to give them each time with him so they could pay their respects.

Sick of being sad, I stopped drinking. I've used the word *stopped* intentionally, rather than the myriad of words available, but that is a private journey, personal choice, and unique story for another time.

It was about this time that I learned that recognizing your feelings have power creates a power all its own. And so I wrote a children's book as a way to redirect my grief from the loss of my parents; being a published author was something my dad always wanted me to accomplish. *What Does Fine Feel Like?* was created. A wink and a nod to the therapists who would never let me get away with fine as the answer to "How are you feeling today?" The book is meant to open a conversation with children about finding words other than *fine* to describe your mood or day.

Right around the time my book was at the publisher, and I was feeling strong and indestructible, the unthinkable happened.

We had just celebrated the end-of-summer party at the lake community we love so much. I had gone home early to get into my pj's, eat some chocolate, and pet my dog. I looked like a total cliché as a group of friends, including my son, Connor, walked in our front door late at night and, as calmly as they could, said, "It's Cammie; she fell. You need to pack; they are airlifting her to Denver."

During the two-hour drive to Denver, all we knew was that our daughter had taken a horrible fall down stairs, had been medically paralyzed, and the paramedics didn't think it was good. We would find out later that, when people asked about her, the paramedics would shake their heads no. Watching the helicopter take off from the field behind the post office in our small town was indescribable. That drive. Oh, that drive. Trying to keep the images away of her in a wheelchair for the rest of her life, imagining what the permanent damage might be...

With my daughter suffering from multiple brain injuries and hooked up to tubes and cords in the ICU, and my husband exhausted after carrying the emotional weight of our family alone for years, I grabbed my son, Connor, and walked him out to the hallway. I asked a simple question, "How are you doing?"

His response? "FINE."

* * *

Have you ever forgotten the combination to a padlock? You try two or three combinations that you *think* it could be, and each time the tug on the handle is met with resistance. Then, a moment you are pretty sure you remember the combination, not one hundred percent certain, but pretty sure, and you slowly enter the three numbers while moving the dial right, then left, then right again. You tug on that handle...and it easily slides open, no resistance. You breathe a little sigh of relief, and maybe even smile.

* * *

"FINE," he said. "Mom, I'm not the one you should be worried about; Cammie doesn't even know what year it is."

Searching for some comic relief, I said something like, "FINE? Your mom is the award-winning author of a book that gives you forty-four different adjectives other than *FINE*, and *FINE* is all you got?"

It opened a conversation with my son, and in that moment I just knew. The combination to the lock just clicked into place. Life has a strange serendipity. I knew Cammie was going to be okay because I had been in an ICU three times in the last four years—once for myself, once for my dad, and once for my mom—and it's hard to explain, but you just *know* what it feels like when the doctors know something bad that you don't. And this wasn't it. (Days later the doctor would remark she really shouldn't have been okay, but that for "some reason" she was going to recover one hundred percent.)

In that moment I also knew that Connor wasn't fine and needed a helping hand to verbalize his fears and how scared he was for his sister. I knew enough about neurological rehabilitation to know Cammie had a long road ahead of her—they didn't need to waste precious time telling me about it because I had lived it—but I also knew that the women in our family are strong AF. I knew I had to be the strong one to give my dear husband, Doug, a break from shouldering the emotional load for years.

I was suddenly acutely aware of how fortunate our family was, even in the face of all of this awfulness, and I knew it was time to dig deep and find my strength. It was time to sparkle again. I knew it was time to seek out the glitter that dusts even the most ordinary of circumstances. I knew everything was going to be okay. I don't know how; I just knew.

I was prepared for a reason.

"

Through my own struggles
of almost losing my voice,
I now empower others to
discover their own.

"

8

Discovering the Power of Your Voice

Lisa Michelle Umina

At the age of twenty-three, I accomplished the milestone of purchasing my first home. Prior to this, I was employed at a local magazine where I sold advertisements, my third career move since graduating high school. My journey to becoming a homeowner was a challenging one. At 18, I moved out of my parent's home and had to work multiple jobs simultaneously to make ends meet and pay for rent and my car payments. It was a valuable experience to learn how to survive on my own.

I picked up shifts at a bar, and I remember I didn't have enough money to order food, so I ate bar olives and oranges for dinner. I worked hard to find job opportunities and was fortunate enough to have two to three possibilities to earn income each month. My friend Tina always found me freelance work. The positions I discovered may not have been my ideal jobs, yet I approached each with a positive attitude, realizing I would gain something valuable from each experience. I quickly comprehended the significance of building connections and remaining open to new possibilities.

It was my hair stylist who mentioned a new opportunity to me. He said he wanted me to meet his friend who owned a magazine company. I did and was offered a sales position. My first few days were tough, trying to figure out how to sell magazine ads, but I loved it! I met so many amazing people. It was the first time I felt like I was doing something I enjoyed. My boss was very motivating and encouraged me to create new concepts for the company. I was top salesperson several times, selling restaurant guides. I always liked the challenge, working as hard to attain the small goals as well as the big ones. I knew it was all about making connections. I enjoyed the lifestyle of having money, enjoying life, and never cutting the budget to buy something I wanted. College wasn't an option, but instead I realized the value of acquiring knowledge through practical experience. I became determined to become an entrepreneur and start my own company, even though I wasn't sure what form it would take. My hard work and willingness to learn from the people and situations I encountered had already brought me success. I was confident that these instincts would steer me towards starting a successful business.

Work wasn't the only thing that stretched my abilities and honed my skills. I loved to have fun, too! When I wasn't on the job, one of my favorite hobbies was singing. Growing up, I loved the weekend entertainment nights my parents shared with us. My dad played the accordion, and my mom sang. My brother and I would dance and sing. These are my fondest childhood memories. Singing was my passion and I performed in church, the school choir, and any school play that had a singing role. Cultivating my singing abilities was a lifelong aspiration of mine.

I wanted to pursue my passion in singing and I hired a vocal coach who encouraged me to take my passion to the next level and try out for the Cleveland Cabaret. On the audition day, I drove around for what seemed like hours, looking for a place to park. Arriving late wasn't my style; the later I was, the more I tried to convince myself to drive home. I kept thinking of a way to get out of auditioning.

I must have said a hundred times, "I am not that great of a singer to sing in this class!" but it was required to be in the Cabaret. Nevertheless, my type of personality is always up for a challenge, so I finally found a parking spot and hurried to the audition.

As soon as I arrived, the professor asked me to introduce myself and sing in front of other performers. Thank goodness, I was allowed to sing with accompaniment and not a capella. I chose the song "Memories" by Barbara Streisand, one of my favorite artists, and one with an incredibly high voice. The pianist queued me to start, and I almost thought I couldn't get the first note out. Barbara sings three-octave, and my voice was a second soprano, but I could reach her range when I sang her songs. To my relief, I did well. The professor said to take a seat, so I guessed that meant I was accepted! For the next several months that followed, I enjoyed the new challenge of taking professional singing lessons and felt pretty cool carrying my leather bag with all my sheet music into the school.

In addition to singing, I had another hobby that I was interested in pursuing but was too scared to try. I wanted to challenge myself and try something new, even if it was difficult. My family and friends often suggested that I should become a comedian. I found a class with a professional comic and began writing short bits and sketches. What I liked about the course was that everything we did was building toward graduation day when we had to perform on stage in front of an audience at Hilarities, a well-established comedy club in Akron, Ohio. I never imagined how hard it would be to put together an eight-minute skit! The teacher was fun, and he gave us all suggestions. He told me, "Make fun of yourself! You have to take yourself apart so that people laugh and not stare at you or the clothes you are wearing." I tried to understand what he meant, but he gave an example of being an Italian woman with prominent eyebrows and a mustache. I almost died. I didn't have a mustache! (Well, I did, but I waxed that thing off every week!) I laugh even now when I think about how I had to include this in my comedy act.

I was so nervous that I didn't sleep the night before my first show. My family was coming to support me, but I almost didn't want them there because I would be mortified if nobody laughed. It has to be the worst nightmare of every comic who fears standing alone onstage, hearing only the sound of crickets. To my surprise, that didn't happen to me, and I was hooked. I continued to practice and write more material.

Coincidentally, my aunt started to work at Hilarities in downtown Cleveland. She said she arranged an audition for me. Wow! I was excited until I realized I was walking into a three-minute act for only the club owner in a dark auditorium with an enormous white light shining directly in my eyes. I had no idea how to deliver my material to one person. It was awkward and so damn scary. Besides saying, "Begin," he didn't say a word afterward, nor did he laugh at my skit. I left the building thinking, "Well, there goes your career in comedy."

Later that evening, the phone rang. It was the bar manager, and he said, "Lisa, we'll see you next Tuesday. You'll be the opener for the show that night." As soon as I hung up, I fell to the ground crying. I couldn't believe it. I was funny! I went on to perform several shows for them and loved my material. I made voice impressions from ET and did a skit from the movie, "My Cousin Vinny," imitating Marisa Tomei. After a while, however, I wasn't having as much fun. I had to follow comedians with some very disgusting acts. One woman's monologue was all about her genitals; my routine wasn't at that level. The bar manager mentioned to me one night that my act was too clean for a club. I stopped doing comedy not long after. I missed performing, but I knew that in addition to singing, I could write and had a good sense of humor.

Time passed, and I put my energy into my work. I began to notice that I started waking up with a sore throat. Usually, after a cup of coffee, I would gain my voice back. But later in the day, when I was talking to my customers or singing, I would lose my voice in the middle of a word or phrase. I started to cough a lot. I didn't know what was happening, but it scared me.

I remember the day at the doctor's as if it were yesterday. He examined my vocal cords by inserting a large, camera-equipped tube down my throat. I grasped for air it was so uncomfortable. It was the most unpleasant exam I had ever undergone. It lasted more than just a few seconds. Although I was treated with a numbing spray, I felt every movement of the tube going down and returning up. But that wasn't the worst part.

The doctor found two cysts on each of my vocal cords. He wanted to run more tests to rule out cancer. I could barely process what he said. Who the heck gets cysts in their vocal cords? He explained that it is common for singers and professional speakers to have polyps on the outside of the vocal cords, which are easier to treat with a laser procedure. Finding cysts inside the vocal cords was different and removing them was even more difficult. If they were cancerous, I would need chemo and radiation. The out-come didn't look promising.

Unbelievably, the tests came back that the cysts were benign. That was a significant relief, but the ordeal wasn't over. The doctor planned to drain the fluid in the cysts. My mind raced. I asked him how my voice would sound after the fluid was removed. He said it would be different and gave me a list of foods and drinks I needed to avoid. One of the drinks on the list was coffee, my favorite beverage, and the caffeine isn't suitable for someone with sensitive vocal cords.

He scheduled the surgery the following week, and the days leading up to it were an absolute emotional roller-coaster for me. In hindsight, I should have seen a counselor. The "what-ifs" were too vast and relentless. "What if I can't talk?" "What if my voice changes?" "What if I don't have a voice?" "Will I sing, and will I sing at the same range?" I cried myself to sleep every night preceding the surgery. When I was awake, I prayed and prayed. I remember one night; I was angry with God; I had many things I still wanted to do and relied on my voice for everything. "Why would He take all this away from me?"

The first surgery didn't work. Draining the cysts wasn't the solution; they filled up with fluid months later. After the second surgery, I had a voice but was told not to use it for two weeks. Me, not talk for two weeks? I was going out of my mind. I wanted to try out my voice to see if it worked. I wanted to know if I could sing again. Despite railing against God, I still had faith and had to rely on it as never before. I awoke every morning before my surgeries and walked to morning mass. I was very involved with my church and loved the peace I felt when I was at mass. During the two weeks, I didn't have my voice; I would sit in the back of the church and remain silent, though not by choice.

At home, I tried to stay busy with crafts and tanning on my back patio. One day I locked myself out. I couldn't call anyone– I could barely whisper. Wearing only my bathing suit, I had to go next door and ask my neighbor to call the locksmith. I can only imagine what my neighbor thought when she came to her front door. Her face said it all. She was so confused as to why I was whispering. I would have no idea if she thought someone was in my house or what. Every time we would see each other afterward, the memory of that situation would cause us both to chuckle.

Those were the longest two weeks of my life. I was utterly bored out of my mind and felt very desperate. So,

I did what most people do when they are out of the office on sick leave. I let myself daydream. My desperation slowly turned the corner and met my creativity. I put some Enya music on, lit some candles, sat down at my dining room table, and started to write. A children's story started to take shape. I wrote, and I wrote. I edited, and I edited. I had piles of crumbled-up paper on the floor. (I wish I had taken photos of this experience. I am sure most writers do the same.) I figured if I had a visual of the main character, it would help me to write the story. I started to draw Milo. Milo stood for "Me Inside, Loving Outside." That's what came to me as I wrote: the story reflected me; all I had experienced and was beginning to understand. The plotline came readily. I loved Dr. Seuss, so I took the challenge to rhyme the story.

In the silence of those days, my heart felt on fire again. Eventually, I would self-publish my first book, *Milo with a Halo*. I went on to create "The Milo and Lisa Show" and performed in schools, libraries, hospitals, churches, and nonprofit organizations. The book sold thousands of copies, and I traveled nationally and internationally. I continued to write children's books, and the third book, *Milo and the Green Wagon* would win a Christian Publisher's Award based on a true story. Through consistent vocal therapy and practice, I regained my voice, although it was altered, over several months. Today, I own my own international publishing company, and I help authors publish their stories. Through my own struggles of almost losing my voice, I now empower others to discover their own.

> I could not do everything myself and that accepting help from people who care about you is not only okay, but necessary and healing.

9

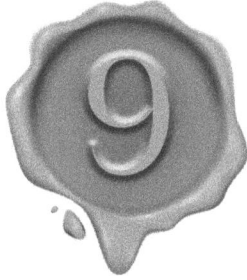

Little Goodbyes

Natalie Wintle

I always knew my parents would probably pass away before me. With that knowledge, I thought I would be ready when that time came. As a registered nurse, I have taken care of many patients during their transition to death. I care deeply for my patients and their families, but I learned to keep professional boundaries so that emotions did not cloud my judgment during their care. I put my emotions aside to do what I had to do. However, that in no way prepared me for when that patient was my father.

I was at work on May 5, 2017, and got a call from my father. "Kiddo, I can't see out of my left eye." He was as calm as I was panicked. He was able to call 911 and was transported to the hospital. This was the day that my whole life changed; I just didn't know it at the time. In December of 2016, my father began experiencing varying symptoms that were becoming more debilitating as time progressed, but doctors were unable to determine a diagnosis. During this time, my sister, my father, and I started calling ourselves the Team because we were working so closely together, and each of us had our own role in the fight. Finally, in April of 2017, he was diagnosed with scleroderma, a disease that causes the hardening and tightening of skin, tissues, and organs. I knew that scleroderma was generally a slow-progressing disease, so I wasn't overly worried. Unbeknownst to us at the time, in my father's case it was aggressive and rapid. My father had given me access to his online medical records, so we could have a better idea of what was going on and track the disease's progress. I took on the responsibility of reviewing each new update, discussing it with my sister who is also a registered nurse, and explaining things in layman's terms so my father would understand.

That phone call in May was the first time I was scared. Up to that point we could manage his symptoms from home, but now it became much more serious. After the initial panic, I went into nurse mode, that emotional dissociation that occurs so you can do your job. I started using my critical-thinking skills to try to determine what happened. The most likely reason was that he'd had a ministroke. We asked the paramedics to take him to the hospital that had the best stroke center. Upon arrival at the hospital, he was admitted to an observation telemetry unit. They did not find anything wrong and recommended that he follow up with his family physician. My sister and I wanted to get something to eat so I went to the nurses' station to see how long it would take for his discharge. The nurse was on the phone with the doctor, getting discharge instructions. She looked at the telemetry monitor and suddenly stopped. She said, "Your father is not going home today; he just went into A-fib." A-fib is an irregular heartbeat that can lead to blood clots and strokes.

He was then admitted to a cardiac unit where he could be monitored more closely. He was in the hospital for seven days, and his strength deteriorated rapidly as many new medical issues arose.

Two days after admission, my father wanted to take a shower. Knowing how overworked hospital staff are, I told him that I would help. Now, that is something I never expected to do, and it felt incredibly awkward. I had showered many of my patients, so I went into nurse mode again.

Thinking of my father as a patient made it a little less uncomfortable.

When they were set to discharge him, I requested a physical-therapy evaluation because I knew he would not be able to take care of himself at home. We were relieved that he met the requirements for admission to a rehabilitation center. The unquestioned expectation was for him to regain enough strength to go home. On May 11, 2017, my father was transferred to a skilled rehabilitation facility. We were all enthusiastic and optimistic about his spending a short time there before going home. My sister and I worked out a schedule in which she would be with him during the day, and I would stay with him in the evenings after I got off work. Physical rehabilitation was scheduled during the day, so I relied on my sister to give me daily updates on his progress. Things did not go as we had anticipated. My father's physical strength deteriorated more rapidly than we could have imagined. Within two weeks he went from walking on his own, to using a walker, to having to use a wheelchair. Watching this man—one of the strongest people I ever knew, a man who could do everything—become so fragile made me feel utterly helpless. I continued to shower him two to three times a week because he said I was the only one who knew how to do it "right." He was unable to walk, so my sister and I assisted with getting him to the bathroom. I also changed the sheets on his bed, ensured everything he needed was within arm's reach and placed where he wanted them, and changed his clothes daily. My sister and I continued to watch all of his lab values and oversee all medical aspects of his care. There were so many things that were out of our control, but we controlled what we could. However, it seemed that for every little step forward, there were four giant steps backward. Two weeks after his admission to the skilled care facility, we realized he kept decompensating. He was in pain and exhausted. He decided he didn't want to continue with the rehabilitation. At that point we spoke to the doctor, and my father entered hospice care. He asked me how long he had left. After watching his labs for weeks and his quickly deteriorating kidney function, I anticipated that he had two weeks. He became very upset. I thought it was because it was such a short time; however, he was upset because he wanted it to be in the next few days. It felt like a literal blow to my chest. The only thing he asked for was that my sister and I spend as much time with him as we could.

My sister and I decided to make the most of the next couple of weeks. In retrospect, it was a way for us to say goodbye, and there were many little goodbyes during that time. My father was coming to terms with the end of his of life, and it was a balance between dealing with his anger at the unfairness and finding peace of mind. The day after my father entered hospice, my sister and I thought it would be best to plan his funeral so we wouldn't have to do it when he passed. Walking into the funeral home was worse than I thought it was going to be. I took a very clinical outlook, just making the decisions I thought my father would want and not thinking of the implications of why we were there. My birthday is at the end of May. When I walked into my father's room on that day, I saw flowers and a card. My father always bought my sister and me flowers and a card for our birthdays, and he didn't want to miss our last one together. He made my sister and me promise we would buy each other flowers from him every year, and we have kept that promise. One day we were at the facility, and it was a gorgeous, bright, warm June day. My sister and I talked him into going for a stroll outside. We wheeled him out, but after just a few minutes my father appeared angry and insisted on going back inside. My sister and I were upset because we saw him just giving up on life. My father had a gold necklace that he had worn every day for over thirty-five years. The day came when he asked me to take it off him and put it on my son. I still remember how it was still warm from his skin as I put it around my son's neck, hands shaking and tears streaming down my face. All the little ways he was letting go broke my heart a bit more.

The day before my father passed, the hospice nurse sat my sister and me down and asked if we were familiar with EMC (Ever More Care). We said that we knew patients were put on EMC when they had twenty-four hours or less before they passed. She said, "Yes, and I am putting your father on EMC." My sister and I were speechless and in complete emotional shock. We were completely unprepared. She then said something that we didn't quite understand at the time—"You need to stop being his nurses and start being his daughters." We stayed with my father for quite a while afterwards. Later that evening my sister called and said her son wanted to see my father, and she wanted me to come too. I was not prepared for how much worse he was from just a few hours earlier. I decided to stay with him that night. I told the hospice aide to wake me if there were any changes. I woke up once during the night, and my father was very restless, so I held his hand and kept telling him I was there. He finally settled down and I went back to sleep. When I woke in the morning, I was absolutely panicked. My father was unconscious and had the worst death rattle I have ever heard. (*Death rattle* refers to the sounds a patient makes as they get close to dying; they are caused by the fluids accumulating in the throat and upper chest.) I yelled at the hospice aide for not waking me, told him he should have woken me, and shouted for him to get out of my way. I was angry and panicked because I knew my father's passing would be very soon, and I felt I had missed precious end-of-life time with my father. I imme-diately called my sister and told her to get to the facility as fast as she could. When she arrived, we sat on either side of my father and held his hands. Within a short time his breathing gradually slowed, and he gently passed away. I felt completely numb.

The first couple of weeks after he passed are still a blur. We went through the necessary motions—notifying family and friends, attending the funeral, dealing with estate issues, etc. There were many tasks that needed to be focused on and completed. After that, I felt a complete shift in who I was. Something fundamental had changed, and I didn't fit into who I was before. It felt as if the whole world had changed, and I was just wandering around lost in it. Nothing was familiar anymore; nothing felt the same.

Prior to losing my father, whenever I heard the word *loss* associated with death, I didn't realize the full extent of that word. I associated it with losing the person. I didn't realize it meant the loss of unconditional support, the loss of their presence, the loss of their being, the loss of their story… Nobody ever told me how crushing the first anniversaries would be. Every first holiday without him, his birthday, the date of his death, every time I did something alone that we had always done together—every one was a crushing reminder he was gone. I had been working part-time as a nurse in a skilled care facility for five years prior to my father's passing. I had taken a sabbatical so I could complete my master's degree, which I received in January 2017.

By that time my father was decompensating so quickly I decided to continue my sabbatical until he was better, never believing that would not be the outcome. After his passing I went back to my nursing career. That only lasted a very short time. Every shift I worked, there was a patient that reminded me somehow of my father, which brought up feelings I had suppressed during my father's illness. I went home emotionally exhausted and cried the entire night. As much as I love nursing and feel it is an integral part of who I am, I realized it was taking too heavy a toll on my mental health. I left and have not practiced nursing since.

Grief inevitably changes people. Even five years later, I have a difficult time being around large groups of people. I still haven't figured that one out. One of the things that I had the most difficult time with prior to my father's passing was accepting help from other people. When my father was in the skilled care facility, I had friends who made sure I ate every day—even going so far as to make dinner for me every evening—friends who always had a bottle of wine available, and friends who were there every day to support me in any way I needed. It made accepting help in a gracious way much easier for me. I realized that I could not do everything myself and that accepting help from people who care about you is not only okay, but necessary and healing. As I look back, I realize I should have let myself feel all the emotions during those months, instead of bottling them up, even though they felt overwhelming. Dealing with them at the time would have been much easier than later all at once.

Grief changes people, and I'm still trying to figure out who I am now. As I read back through this, it sounds so unemotional and clinical. But that is how I was able to handle everything that happened. I miss my father deeply every day, and my heart still hurts.

About the
Authors

Roberto Alfaro was born in New York City and raised in the South Bronx, where he lived for twenty-four years before moving to Connecticut to become a Hartford police officer in 1979. He retired in 2000 after twenty-one years of dedicated service in the patrol division, on the recruitment team, in the mounted unit, and on plainclothes details. In 2020, he also retired from Quinnipiac University as a public safety officer. Today, Roberto continues to enjoy his retirement by working as a professional model, actor, salsa dancer and instructor, motivational speaker, inventor, and writer! He currently resides in Hamden, Connecticut, with his beautiful wife and four children.

Suggested Reading

- *An Officer's Mission To Pay it Forward*
- *Never Stop Dreaming, because No Dream Is Too Big to Dream!*
- *Paying the Miracle Forward*
- *Inspired to Make a Difference*

Susan Eileen is a retired teacher and aspiring author who currently resides in Broadview Heights, Ohio. She is over three years sober and is encouraging people to discover who they really are after losing a portion of their lives to addiction. Susan is an avid reader and quilter; she enjoys traveling in her free time. Susan has a very full life now and looks forward to spending time with her grown children and their husbands. She can be found on TikTok under @soberqueenofhearts and on LinkedIn under Susan Dent-Brown.

In addition to being Mom to her four amazing boys, **Natalie Zangara Friedl** holds a master's degree in nonprofit management and has spent the last twenty-five years working with mission-driven organizations, supporting their human resources, management, strategic planning, and fundraising efforts. Born and raised in Cleveland, Ohio, she is proud to be working with PCs for People, a national organization that reduces e-waste through the refurbishing and recycling of technology, while bridging the digital inequities through the offering of low-cost devices to underserved and unserved populations.

Scarlett Green-Wright lives in Houston, Texas, with her husband, Harry Wright; daughter, Zoe Moody; and twin boys Max and Zeke. Scarlett and her coauthor, Natalie Zangara Friedl, grew up together in Cleveland, Ohio. Having attended school together since sixth grade and graduated from West Geauga High School in 1994, the two of them and their tribe have remained like sisters. The experience shared is a true account of a mother's love that could not possibly be written alone during a time of such pain. This moment is shared in the hopes that it moves you to love bigger.

Crista Salvatore is a global leadership facilitator, executive coach, author, and the founder of Spark Truth (www.sprktruth.com). For over fifteen years, Crista has taught professionals how to discover their authentic style through expanding self-awareness, leveraging their strengths, and increasing their capacity to take action. Her focus is on well-being and authenticity, fully engaging the client and helping them tap into their natural leadership style. Working with Crista, clients develop a holistic view of themselves, which improves their presence and impact. Crista is passionate about her own growth and transformation; she lives a fulfilling life with a focus on connection and love.

Cammie Smith is a first-time author. She lives in Colorado with her parents and brother, and attends Montana State University, majoring in business. She enjoys skiing, photography, and the outdoors. Cammie experienced an event that changed the lens through which she views life, which in turn created this narrative to share with others.

Award-Winning Author

Sabrina VanDine Smith is a children's book author, Gen Xer, and lover of sparkle. She was raised in Southern California, but calls Colorado home, where she lives with her husband and two children. She loves lake life, creative writing, geocaching, cooking, and amateur photography. She was either a gossip columnist or a private investigator in her former life. Though Sabrina's long career as a salesperson was inspired by her dad, being a mom and wife feeds her soul. Sabrina lost both of her parents during the pandemic. Like many Gen Xers, she explored how to name her feelings much later in life. That journey inspired this story.

Award-Winning Author

Lisa Michelle Umina is the founder and CEO of Halo Publishing International, a company that has been in operation since 2002. She also established Hola Publishing Internacional as its sister company. Lisa, who is an award-winning author herself, provides coaching to fellow writers on publishing their own books and developing lucrative public speaking careers. She shares the tactics she has used to achieve success. Lisa is the author of the award-winning book "Milo and the Green Wagon," and the host of the "Award-Winning Authors" podcast.

Natalie Wintle, a registered nurse, was born and raised in Northeast Ohio and has worked at the Veterans Affairs Medical Center for the past thirty-three years. She holds an associate of applied business in computer science technology, a bachelor of science in nursing, and a master of science in nursing education. She is an avid reader and an accomplished cross-stitcher. She loves to travel and has been on thirteen cruises. After taking a break from learning Spanish, she is once again studying the language and hoping to become fluent. Natalie's greatest joy in life is being a mother and grandmother.

PCs for
People

PCs for People is a national nonprofit and e-waste recycler working to get low-cost quality computers and internet into the homes of individuals, families, and nonprofits with low income. By recycling and then refurbishing computers, PCs for People provides a valuable service to businesses, families, and the planet by keeping computers out of land-fills and repurposing them to advance digital inclusion.

Since 1998, PCs for People has become a national leader in digital inclusion by serving over 650,000 individuals, providing 250,000 home computers, connecting 90,000 households to the internet, and responsibly recycling over 13 million pounds of electronic waste through the secure e-waste recycling service.

To learn more visit www.pcsforpeople.org.

Halo
PUBLISHING
INTERNATIONAL

Halo Publishing International is a hybrid publishing company that combines the best aspects of traditional publishing and self-publishing. Our company aims to provide a flexible and affordable publishing options for authors who want more control over the publishing process while still receiving professional editing, design, and global distribution services. Halo Publishing International offers a wide range of publishing packages and services to suit different author needs and budgets, including editorial services, cover design, book formatting, printing, distribution, and marketing. With a focus on quality, integrity, and innovation, Halo Publishing International has helped numerous authors achieve their publishing goals and reach a wider audience.

OUR HISTORY

Halo Publishing International, our mission is to empower authors to share their stories worldwide. Since 2002, we have helped thousands of authors turn their ideas into published books that reach audiences globally. No matter the genre, whether it be science fiction, religious, children's literature, or an instruction manual, Halo Publishing International is dedicated to providing the editorial support needed to make your book a success.

OUR MISSION

Halo Publishing International is a self-publishing company that publishes adult fiction and non-fiction, children's literature, self-help, spiritual, and faith-based books. We continually strive to help authors reach their publishing goals and provide many different services that help them do so.

We do not publish books that are deemed to be politically, religiously, or socially disrespectful, or books that are sexually provocative, including erotica.

Halo reserves the right to refuse publication of any manuscript if it is deemed not to be in line with our principles.

Follow us on our social media
HaloPublishingInternational

To know more about Halo Publishing International please visit
www.halopublishing.com

www.ingramcontent.com/pod-product-compliance
Lightning Source LLC
Chambersburg PA
CBHW050012090426
42733CB00018B/2648